Of Course

Cover design by Thomas Wagster

Published in the United States by

Fence Books
110 Union Street
Second Floor
Hudson NY 12534

www.fenceportal.org
518-567-7006

This book was printed by Versa Press www.versapress.com
and distributed by Small Press Distribution www.spd.org
and Consortium Book Sales and Distribution www.cbsd.com.

Library of Congress Control Number: 2020932453

Wagner, Catherine (1969–)
Of Course / Catherine Wagner

ISBN 13: 978-1-944380-16-8

First Edition
10 9 8 7 6 5 4 3 2

Fence Books are published with the support of all Friends
and Members of Fence.

Of Course

Catherine Wagner

FENCE BOOKS
HUDSON NY

Contents

for the critters, especially Ambrose

For whom
it may concern

Bunny slippers made
of real bunnies

would be warm
and tragic

Would they be alive?
Not for long

though they would be
warmer if they were alive

Warmer for whom?
Think of the bunnies try to

think of others, all
fur you.

Will not try to make love

with your specific muscular bottom
but with a general generalized beautiful

world bottom.
Will generalize
the commandingly yeasty smell I get
from my cunt and from bread.
Will not root into sweaty place
where leg meets groin
on anyone specifically other to me.
Trees have groins too.
Cathedrals do.

Round pond frozen over, swathed in snow.
My glasses keep fogging up
to generalize ego relation so
I take you all as one!
hide my tall purple shadow
in taller tree shadow
to remove observer from scene.
The wind makes warm

obstruction out of me.
Somewhere down in a buttcrack
a valve pushes out soft cakes
of matter, valuable
bacteria communities—
"The Martian" in the movie needed
the asses of his friends
for their shit not for their beauty
and he grew potatoes
to prove that a white man alone
may rule a planet
through sheer ingenuity!
and millions of dollars' worth of equipment.
Hey other bottoms

clothed against the cold,
dimpled, carven, cleanly pooping,
cellulitey, and precoded
with cheap unhappy heuristics:
skin-color, cunt or cock—
You don't show your bottom
unless you feel safe
or are forced.

Got snow in my boots,
I didn't tie them tight.
Saw sun and snow
landing on the bottom of the world,
far down as they
can go

the snow landed,
it was grounded, very
grounded snow,
that knew its place and shone there.

Now I'm like shouting at the march
"*No one to be a bottom*
except by choice!" and "*No*
to being grounded"
if the grounds for it are
not—…if you've just

settled.
I am walking away
from my bottom
and it follows me like the moon
makes my blood boil.

Collapse feeling

into expression.
Suck expression through address.

Roll address along the dolly of convention.
Skip heart.

Imagina (rhymes with "vagina"?)
the Experience!

Write What Is and What Isn't and What May Be.
Is there anything else or will that do?

English is 99% buckled to a rock

Should we change language
In sedimentary, metamorphic, or igneous fashion

I propose to yoke it
To the underside of a life

Also to the inside and the other side of the life
We can attach English anywhere

For like an emotion or a military rank
English takes up no space

But my voice exists in time and space
A public-private partnership

It hums out local air that's moved
Presumably everywhere

Full of yeasts and stream toxins
Egg in its testes like an Ohio frog

How to make a poem to communicate using electronic mind-meld apparatus

Try to think rough patterns around the breath
—zigzags of green interlarded with a cumming feeling

plus bitter garland/undersmoke of
"I'm too young for this."

Try nonsonic rhyme, lighght
slowed down to haptic—

Anyway don't use
the kind of known language I'm now using.

At any moment a poem might be riven
by lightning/smell

of burnt sugar (onion?).
Will there be puns and homonymic

play? sure, we can say *door/dour*
and make it taste like coffee or how

popping out of the toaster
feels to live bread. Total poetry!

A poem till now couldn't try to know
how you were doing, real time

ask or hear/respond.
With brain-meld apparatus,

no need to ask, no need
to take turns. As toaster/toast

we simulcast united, author-free.
May peace be with you.

But may also
also be with you.

How else will our fictions
feel their way past one another's

Wet & Wild camembert
lipstick/internet bridges over

troubled trolls/incest-colored hy-art/
racist scaffoldings/soft grizzled hair

on middle-aged men's napes/
glitter rising underwater

when the poem's spanked?
Separate you, misunder-

stood, did raise blisters on my brain
I popped by nuzzling head into a pig

whose gun shot blank blank verses.
Though rarely did I cop to violence.

That's over. We're together now.
Yet under new mindmeld regime

forced empathy
could become hatred factory—

sharers gathering, as before,
in groups rubbed wrong-same-way

until they form and live
inside a blister.

Outside of blister-atmosphere
(which is drown-juice):

dry cold air
no one knows how to breathe.

We'll build escape route
infra-real, through form! try

fixed pattern interrupted,
classic tactic

for arresting attention,
this time done with *feeling*:

I'll share a
spoon of kiss,

8 times; then
fork of kiss, 4 times—

finally,
spork of sick

twice, spork of sick—
a synthetic surprise

doubled down on
loudly to ring.

That's the form or frame.
We'll put whatever we want

to get across in there and it will smell
like kiss, kiss who, my ass, ma,

a word for unpleasant confused
discharge.

Done with words.

Hinges

Rhymes not split apart by
Time will go raw and unheard. A

Name or a color applied to a surface will
Mime for its

Framers its being for them.
Blame hangs on a line between

Aim and result. A
Game without

Time can't be fixed and a
Game without players is fair.

Poem for an Anthology

Maybe it's for an anthology about dogs
so here is a dog
dog go oof

Maybe it's for an anthology about "men"
who are "dogs"
—sniff around, take a piss, move on

Maybe it's for an anthology
about smells
a housekeeping anthology
about how to get rid of smells

Maybe it's for an anthology about gender
about how to get ripped in or off in it

Maybe it's for an anthology
about how to smell
not from the smeller's point of view
but from the smell's point of view

and from the smell's point of view
which is objectively diffusing
look at that—

good evening—pissed off
doesn't have a smell

Rising action

The horizon gave head to the sun
like guillotine.

The other side of the planet
staged an uprising

nightfall.
A protocol called friction

made our breath audible.
Narrative curved along our muscles

provoked them to stretch
this and that way at work.

They had gentled the boy inside the girl
till the girl was basic.

They had gentled the girl inside the boy
till the boy was basic

and riding fascist genitals
felt like rowing.

Though 4 out of 5 girls weren't raped
the history of mammalia

was a history of penetration
and we were getting bored

(a) through or (b) of it.

You are

foreclosed not by my senses five

my senses five deliver
all you are to me
to me

but there's more you that's not for me—
not closed to me nor open to me
but twisted into focus by other lenses.

Just look at you, my girl. They do.

Wood steel brick sheetrock

Trained to quadrant. Quadrants
Reign, manage space, rot in
Rain, bugs chew on them, my
Home spongy from carpenter ants
Tombed in turn when
Rain floods their nest and out of
Room up through my floor their corpses
Drown. A little
Doom shared among animals, my
Broom caressing ants near open window
Fame of sun, birds gossip in it, bright red
Male on treetop sings of happy larder
Town or brokedown
Dream of representing cheer or
Demon plan to organize the birds in
Formations inhuman.
Rime denotes the changes
Rung on denotative
Lines I mean to drape with a
Drone mood that checks in with its
Roaming sensors
Only once a second. Surveillance feeling
Tonal but is structure bound.
Lo, Ohio.

Of Course

Fweep or ckkkk from
trees tall grasses shrubby clumps
loud chirrup or scratch-bell
scifi laser pew pew pew

at borders   between properties

But when I steal across the golf course lawn
no singers

live in lawn maybe earthworms
moles bugs voles nematodes but
no singers are going to live there and
get mowed. Or all of them got mowed.

In the periphery I was secret gong
hanging the hammock thinking CALL MY MOM
not doing that or any other task ha
HA I'll do my job of

putting head outdoors   the garden ringing
unfocused my eyes allowed
  moving shadows on the lawn
                like baby whales playing 20 feet underwater
  to shift their noons

Sun on green leaves brings out their yellow
  My eye drags tree to sky, prints violet margin

Still a little way from trash-thicket
                back of golf course
let's go IN there   into buzzing silver haze-lasso

dang it I can never see the crickets.
Squatted by pond to spot a couple of disco frogs and a cricket I thought
was very close. I didn't see any of them but did see spider, tiny beige, tie
a web between grasses. The frogs talk, maraca speed slowing to plucked-
string: "That's -how-it-is; that's how it—is; is is—that's how it is is is is—
that's   how it is. That's how—it is."

We get the notebook out
like we used to do.
Want to catch a cricket.

Do you want to come and say goodbye
to me? I would treat it like your birthday,
beautiful—spoil you rotten, fuck you so much,
bite your big lips. Just want to
chew on your ginormous lips
forever, kiss and coo.

No edge to cricket-noise
gathers elsewhere to me.
Outside in a dirty white deer-printed t-shirt
letting the cricket-jangle be.

I could try to reflect the world back on itself—
  I can't though, position alters view—so if position alters view,
what do you see, small-town mom poet
  at decent regional university?
That poetry at the university
  helps brand the institution
as more than philistine, and it is
  my inside job to rehearse the free discourse
a university permits. But we can't say
  "post-growth" in the title of our speaker series
or funders will run away.
  And spoken word's not spoken here;
it's too direct (to be direct: this lab's
  whites-mostly).

Spilled beer on me
  I smell like microbrewery
bought by corporate and told stay free, be
  what metrics are measured against.
Take poetry away and data fetish fills the lab,
  admin backs up out of the smoke hood
you'd put your head in to protect yourself.

                    Tense patterned turmoil of crickets   too large to track,
       can't see them working, how they respond to one another, how they group.

                                        Pond still. Swallows wheel
                                   reflected in trees and sky below
                                        Six Canada geese
                                          frogs, crickets,
                                          human popsong
                                          "Crazy in Love"
                    from the PA at golf course swimming pool near road.
           Built with public funds in 1934 by the WPA and the Kiwanis Club,
                          it was once the city pool, for whites only.
        In 1949, members of the Oxford, Ohio NAACP sued for desegregation.
        When the NAACP won, the city arranged for ownership to "revert"
                          to the private Golf Club, expanding it into
                          a whites-only Country Club. The city didn't build
                          the new public pool (over on Fairfield)
                                   till 1974.   Chorus/refrain.

                                             Swallow
                                     blows in triangles
                                    folds and reappears.
                          I fling some snot into the grass.
                             Looks like insect eggs.
                                    Fuck off work,
                             the grass blows seeds
                                in sun and breeze.
              Some algae has detached from the edge of the pond
                          and floats in little islands.

Fell asleep on a rock
Now it's raining a bit
So I will walk
The clicka frogs are chorusing
Communicating what
Think like a frog
But man's calling his dog—"*Mindy!*"
He sounds impatient—I would not want
to go back to him either.
Can't see well with left contact
And I do not have a project
stepping slowly on brown earth   between
blurred irregular   ranks of green
virginia creeper   poison ivy

ground crickets
begin their ululant rotating pauses
I get married to this

shimmer shaketting inside itself coalesces
into pulse   foreground background
Let me see you crickets!
The chorus has swollen—not yet a roar
From PA: "…*I find you and hold you down (Miss Sing Sing)*"

—That's "Hold Up,"
in which Beyonce takes a power stance, dom stance,
while admitting that her monogamous demands make her a prison—
"Miss Sing-Sing." Which does not mean Jay-Z is not a jerk.
Nevertheless, she's "miss-Sing" him.
Not to be outdone, she, too, will go missing.
She knows he's going to miss her more.
That's how she'll hold him down.

Haven't seen any people since
I went off course.
Red-winged blackbird other side of pond,
twerpy buzzsaw.

Geese.
Ground crickets, handsome trigs.
Cardinal
birdy-birdy,
liquid loose. A rabbit.
A fawn switching its tail, neck
glows in sun.
Starlings gather in one of the
unleaved trees, a dead
ash tree. Fuck you
emerald ash borer.
Ash leaflets repeated themselves
lined up, busy, back and forth,
"   "" " —they rolled their r's
and bristled. That's what they used
to do.
Repeat, bristle. Ash.

Went down to get notebook
sleep is for poured concrete
The cat has sprayed
in the living room, I can't see where
Hello "god" cricketsound silvery fractal
apparently tireless   they
sing all night   they do not clean their house   they eat
and marchingly, without moving forward,
rub hairy legs   together
When I write I play my body too
Require a tool

The main golf course:
land laid out, curved by dozers
tailored, tricked-out, lawned-over,
intentionally
moved, maintained,
weeds killed
a mile down Four-Mile Creek
Versus

land in back
of course:
mounded logs, broken concrete,
earth-piles
abandoned, furred over
side-lit, flooded gold

Moving air redirects around
my face and body (feel it more on my exposed face)

All minutes of the land, all millimeters
have own intelligence and agenda
in combination and in relation

Crush the plants in the path
with boots, and hardy weeds
pop up next to the path, the ones
that love disturbed soil, the healing plants.

I like damaged people,
people who complain
Get bored by healthy-minded
denizens of the mowéd plain
Prefer sturdy grousers, weeds, nutrient-rich
gossipers, anarchists of the
roadside, who grow in the ugly
complaint the floor of action.

An I was built to rip a
we apart?

Create
remonstrable success. Remonstrable outcomes.

Posing with my face in hall in hell-hello
like a dolphin in spring
(mid-spring) I nose the office air
and space haunts where I was.

To open a space behind me,
I go.
To offer space beside me
is harder,
I scribble in the air in living space
that stinks of cat litter.
To make a space in front
of me is hardest—
I'm going that way
you're
there already?
could run you over.
I'll follow quietly.
To make a space inside
of me I breathe my [b]other.

> A silent person   everglade
> Crickets, birdsong, squirrel, wind
> Sit in green in
> Body breasts legs
> Big dumb ears that cannot isolate crickets
> Shooter killed 49 at Pulse nightclub Orlando
> Just sitting here is ok srsly
> Rough grass   Go ahead and rise, panic.
> You are a wish for love
> So love.

> The pond went Sparkle Sparkle
> then wind laid pond's belly hollow
> and the sparkles died
> Then an unwind Sparkle Sparkle

Ha ha — I am home and
It calls itself it
It gonna go crazy her
It live her by itself
and with hi, its child, hi hi he

It is very tired, too tired to write
it produces
silence on the lam.

> The mist moves, it has no destination,
> it is part of the mist.
> Which will decay in sun.
> The wind that pushed the mist
> wrinkles the pond—
> all but the tallest of the upside-down
> trees now obscured. The mist
> still arriving in slow carriages.

> What nucleates sky ice
> for cloud formation?
> Plankton poop,
> dirt-sized, caught up in mist.

> Build heaven of excrement
> that engines [*v.*] rain [*n.*].

Look outside into yard
see the growing not the "weeds"
which are to-do list/shame
I put on airplane mode
Put on do not disturb
Stand and look at the yard/world
Weedy, with daylilies
and a holler tree, so I should holler.

> Cricketsong firmly established—one *hzzzh*
> high thick thick high fence.
> Now I hear inside it 8–10 pulses per second,
> high low points of different singers' songs
> intersecting in acidic thrum.
> Some are silent, foraging or breeding
> in my ears   a version of forever.

I know verbs move

a line, but
nothing   here is moving
Stop in the path.
Sun strikes
a log through trees.
Bird: Great news. Great great
great—
Approach page scared
Pileated woodpecker
drumming on a dead ash tree.

We don't follow the law of conservation of angular momentum because
    it's a law,
we follow it because we can't help it
and we don't not murder because murder is against the law
we, we, we, we, we
murder anyway, we do what we think we have to
embezzle tort trump property lump.
I'm my bitch, I'm my
bitch! I'll have
feedback to you ASAP.

Wherever I stop, the closest cricket also stops. I am a threat.
Crouching in tall grass to spot them, in amongst them, still
can't see them (see other bugs—wasps spiders flies beetles).
The sound changes as I turn my head—
diffuse and angular ringing buzz
spills over horizon-dam
surrounding town

Stay silent till you know you're safe, crickets
till you know the others are safe

of course   but whenever possible please be calling to your others

Man at nature fest
displayed crickets he'd collected in Butler County (here)—
dozens of species pinned under glass, large and tiny, Ohio colors, green
    and mud
Hey I can't even collect ONE, have only ever scouted one by ear
(handsome trig, underside of honeysuckle leaf, Hilltop Road)
though I stare and stare
Excuse me sir how the— "You go out there" he says
"With a flashlight and a net"
I try, I lie down under bushes
Oh well I don't want to pin them down
just want to visit with them
I'm not the lady they want, I get close to one it goes silent
though the rest take up the slack, sing my hearties
keep up the good work everyone
I'm going back to the office

Snaggled some time to write
  Stole it from the truth   My gosh! it's the OUTSIDE
                                                        Insane air pump

                                                Back among the crickets
                                             continuous all separately
                                                             start stop

Cicada interlude
I have 9% charge left
for recording silversonic trampoline size of whole rec center
Yard shaketty with *Neotibicen tibicen tibicen*
big low burrr, high filigree response
In the Stevens' yard a huge and scary cage
degrades, sly, maybe sinister, and reinflates
Swamp cicada near Clyde's yard doesn't care what the others say
works at the high edge building a net of filament.
Other cicadas crust the net with broken pearls

decorate it higher than the template.
Magicicada wave summits over Kelly's yard, divides into whizzy shakings
that pass through one another,
transparent fabric leashed
to insect chests.
A bird joins.
Phone dies.

                              Dried clover-flower on its stalk
                            green center, white-rimmed, thin
                           brown wrinkled petals starring out,
                       brown hooks pointing in different directions
                          at the crimped thin end of each petal.
                                 A record of expansion.
                                Expansion is star-shaped
                            if one's reach is not obstructed.
                             Shape of firework, classic
                                  articulated bloom,
                          "operates according to a logic of"
                            Spread arms, lie back on grass

                               Went to school in the tree
                            I like to xylem and phloem till we
                               push a seed out the stem.
                                      That's gross.
                        Seed gets a message, pollination, "time
                                 to become a billion
                                 bigger than you are"
                               big bang happens daily.
                                 Xylem and phloem
                                Jailem and drownem
                               Kingdom and file 'em

                     Fell asleep. Geese crossed pond. Monde.
                             My feet sweating in boots.
                             Sun lower, wind rising.

A gesture, grass upside-down.
I gesture of
Dead, tree head in the water

Well I don't want any more to get   in translucent
pond past wet.

Red poppies holding the light, someone's yard.

Driveway cracks (mine). Kill the weeds.
Cut their throats. Drink their blood.

Late cricket shoots light-hyphens from a space-gun
and the victim day is permanently charged.

I've had an excellent walk
Sudden urge to get married
to the day.
Get married to my life
and have a lifely life
whose isn't any else I own.

Try with and without an us.
Without an anus
mouth's no help.
But a mouth is helpful.
Kiss the anus too.

December, marching
to keep warm, heading back.
I swear I hear crickets,
dim silvery ringing
—"snowy crickets"?
continuous overtone
fry of
neural activity/
blood traffic?
message
echoes land-shape.

The bitch sleep still curled up in child's pose
other side electrified fence

                                        Mom's getting a defibrillator
                                             pen out of juice
                                           trees no leaves yet
                                            clumpy gray sky
                          upside-down trees in runoff pond
                            calm doublings. Sitting on log,
                                         boots in swamp.
                                    Leaves in melt puddle
                               beech, oak, are soft-silted,
                           funged over, mossed, can't see
                                       edges, unshapes
                                         I could name
                                arendt-bloat, farleigh,
                          soft-boat, softclaws, mud galaxy,
                          smoking clot, feinted burrow. Not
                          going to look the same tomorrow.

                       Pond close to the road gray-green
                  and the upside-down trees sharp. Hear
        HVAC   cars
             exhaust

                    culvert—
                       stream through it.

My Hair Is Getting a Free Blow Dry in the Win

and great, was listening to one from Bernadette
where she says "Let's get back to our unpaid work as always"

and my hair is dry for
my hair is frozen   I said *for*

not for   the thing you row a boat with
but not spelled like that kind of for   shit I said OR.

Wind eats water even when it's cold.
Wouldn't snow get eaten then by air? It does.

Time doesn't have edges except when you count it up.
I do much enjoy walking and along way

I said a long way I like it in the sun and cold and
walking arcs and divides time

in a fashion appropriate to the size of my body.
You can pile up all the money   it's countable

but every piece of it gets bigger
or smaller in comparison to other currency,

no absolutes   so money stretches wrongly
around time stretched by working legs.

I could buy you a drink and you would say Thank you
for the drink has a glass border

so we can count it   have another
stop counting   get to a

time we stop punching in.
When I dictate   data flies up to satellite

and is instantly returned bioprocess inappropriate
to the size of my body

or making nonsense of the idea that anything is
appropriate or inappropriate to the size of my body

it feels good to have the
satellite bounce words   by a process

my friend dear friend was fucking me this morning so sweetly and I feared
in the middle of so sweetly gently that we were boring maybe

to be so gentle. But it's not for me boy
I said not for me boring because it gels me to the interior soup

as grease forms in the fridge on soup, you slowly gently
warm it so your spoon won't break soft carapace

melted. It's not because we/we're fucked
that I try to dictate   I think to say this wrongly

preserve cold Oxford for our ancient death.
Unseasonable cold in Oxford

Oh hi   o the border of cunt lucky
swayed by current juiced from glacier and

through the great lakes twisting a hoard
of wind. Thank you.

Fantasizing during

Revisited "bad priest & fat-breasted
Suburban girl"

Edges swell toward coming
Flesh toaster stuffed with hard oily pillow
A rotten sundown mouse   is elongating   dripping fur
Shoved out of town   on soft and distance rail

Move the skin aside
And in the tent find
Things to say and eat

As long as she thinks it's
Good it's going to work

Questions or Quatrains

Pregnant with death   till I die
And am delivered
Of   whatever got me pregnant
Hand terribly asleep

I kiss you hundred times
I kiss you more
Cervix migrated to where it gets banged on, hurts
I wanted coffee

My guy clung to doing right thing, his
Make-up round, or test
Flung me on flights in the mundane
Sheets very stained

I flooded them. Plus blood
From period. *Of* is
Abstract louche connector
From's in time, starts

Where things used to be
I also too was from
Time in folds of field or flesh
Prodded my flagpole there

Oh he moved, a shock of warm
Gold clock of name
Anchored my ice
He keeps on being temporary

I am thought of not comfortably
Must give more comfort
Lower back now pressed to his
In my from is

The labor that I do
In time in front of you
You ascend to audience/audensity
As I commit our boundary

The moon has a body

The moon has a head but no body
So why assume [she]
Is cold why not
Assume drunk
"Legless"
She can keep up pretty good though
With my car in the rural night
Fantasy in which
I am a passenger
My left leg lolls and
My friend reaches a hand
Across the emergency brake
Which points now at the base of
The gearstick shaft
And *can* point at its head
But nowhere else
Thus does not
"Speak"
And unless overused abused is
Reliable
Whereas anyone can misunderstand
Or willfully misinterpret the
Point and represent
Are very different (Moon!)
6am and the snow
Sent enough light upward
For this window to
Transmit and permit
My seeing
I heard more than I saw
I understood less than I heard
I was well read compared to
But not compared to
I begin to feel warm in
My crotch, as if a wodge

Of moist electric blanket
Were stuck in there
And my friend was not
Riding on the other side of the brake
—I mean emergency—he is not
Fox-hunting and on
A horse in a novel
In which the brake
Is a strip of greenwood
He is downstairs the coffee's
Made but he ignores
My text   He works alone
And I will have to go down there

Not drunck at all   Amtrack Hudson–Penn

If you're put in exactly
the same mood as me
when you get this
the poem is a fascist

desire   OK
because impossible like
beating interiority out of exteriority
won't clear a channel

Cri de/off course

Want to feel flame tide up and float me
In fat
Chew
Away
Shun
Love

I don't care what you object are
Can I just *feel that*
Even knowing you are wrong and bad for me
Even knowing you are boring

Little tiny poem
Give me aid
Your letters flash
Up on the scree

Cantell u to come
You know I'm so slow
What person is going to
Touch me like you
Clever beddle down
Light fingered
Howd you do
It it it it it it it it
With your stubby fingers

Fingers in me
Mad me weep spume
Haha, you felt a
Ha the wet brokade

The new one
Makes you feel safe
She likes she don't unlike

What you show
She won't
Knock you stiff
With her lizard tail
Like didn't I
You don't
Like that any more?
You never know what I am
Going to say to
Yaaaaaaaa
Open cavern of dismay dimsaid
Who could
Stand up in there?
Plus lethal lizard
Swerves back to attack

No that I am
Eld and wiz,
In no why to do
Just love a you

I got more than some people I had a pretty man
I got a little house my own money
I don't shit in the sink I
Raise son try
How do it
Fucking work
It feels like home
Don't cheat it
Rose hell
I like to rose hell He'll

Not love me
We fucked and bodyloved
But I can do without
My gemmy carton florid muck
Sore hack

Sorry but
I thought I was too interesting for u
But I was terribly snobb wrong snubby dogscruff

Can I be queer nope I'm pretty straight
I am into that one woman tho, with the nape of her
Sloth on her, damp slow
glassette oer her labia
Crawl in marsupial
Rue pocket like hey how you
Doing being done
By me
Do you rue you rude
Smack tits small tits for a
Secretly mouthy
Sucker?

Yeah you are fucked up
Are you wise no
Yeah fuckup
Kissed by a lossy old girl

If you want lossless performance
Keep expectations lo-fi
I got away
From what I didn't want
His strange ratcheted frequency
A thick buzzing wire
It was semi hard
To extract myself
Easy, one sleepless night
Thinking about a blonde in his bed
Got me out of him

Anybody gonna want me?
Hi I am sane
Clean like the Amazon

After a rain
It rains all the time
It kicks up the mud
Clean mud, garbage
You can't see through it
Piranhas climb up your pee stream
When you pee into it

Well that's aggressive and uncalled for
Who did anything to you
For you to go so phallic-harm
O single mom

Q:—To charm or harm
the instantiation of the phallus
that presents itself
to the Single Mom?

A:—No power, no harm
No wower
No be wowing
Home with you
From work it's dark
Make something quick
To eat for son
Eat for son

Look how I go on
When pain is personal to me
Go and be ordinary
Haply happily and safe
The usual harm please only
Nothing better

"Woman unmissed how you crawl to me crawl to me"
Nah that's not
Not how I do

SIX VERY SHORT POEMS ABOUT SKETCHUAL VIOLETS

for AC and the others

1. *Toothless Imperative*

She took the streetcar to high school
in Baltimore (virgins, nuns),
was gang-raped in community college
by a professor and a group
of his male students,
was raped again after Peace Corps,
when she didn't want to go home
to her dad (who'd beaten her
for being raped), so she'd
joined a Peruvian circus
to hang by her hair,
raise spangly legs.
Don't do that—
be a virgin? study with nuns?
raise spangly legs? hang by hair?—
don't have kids if you do?
Don't be raped.

2. *Gothic song (after de Nerval)*

Sweet bride
I love your crying!
Its rain
Scents the flowers.

Sweet things
Bloom once.
Let us sow roses—
They go with time!

Dark or blonde—
Must one choose?
The God of the world
Is Pleasure.

3. *Don't like this*

Can taking be made safe
Can having be unharm
Can unharm sexy be
And having limits, probed?/Am having limits, prone?

I felt terribly touched when you

Don't drink like that
Don't parody your mouth
Don't like or be

Like May came out of me
I was dismayed

4. *Sketchual Violets*

I'm at table, drawing—
Someone says "Baby

Do you want to sketch
Some Violets"

I don't say no
Who'll pay for

Bruisy violets
Mixed media

5. *The Trial*

My terrible
Recunting of
The story to control a self
My terrible
Recunts until

"*Unhamlich!*" says the judge ("Fake meat!").

So I'll tell you myself:
Recant cuntrol.

6. *We keep our great bodies safe (Mike Hunt is in the building)*

I enter the rose garden, a leisure place
the park designer's name is Law
PROVEN WINNERS
COMPACT PINK INNOCENCE
to write by the little
Olmsted lake fuckoo
I mean it's very nice I like it poetry
for men die every day for lack
of what is found there?
women don't have time to die for that?
I totally have time this week
to say unfair to men and passing fair
Mike Hunt's a walking mist, a starry mist
that labels no man's dream

I was raping things that didn't matter

not as a way of disciplining them
but to comfort myself, to establish
my way as the highway. How great
to seek comfort where nothing
seems to hurt, I damage innocently,
in no sense
can I be wrong.
As a babe I sucked my mother's breasts
and they were sore, they cracked
and when I pulled the plastic off
the ears of corn lying on green styrofoam
or lying on the nonproprietary
name for styrofoam, because
I prefer to anchor
my talking in a thing unbranded—
though things I rape
are branded as not mattering
in the/my perceivable grid,
and when I turn them to use
I do so privately, a pleasure to
spread their green slits with my fingers
and move inside of them, and do it
again—and when the ears of corn
came off the stalk
a chemical signal alarmed
right down to the roots, and signaled
an increased absorption
of water through the xylem
—live in the world and hurt
the living lining, that's how
I paid down debt
when I was tied spreadeagled
to the blades of a huge steel fan.
My soft teardrop boobs hung down.
A field of babies on the gym floor
needed to be fed
and I was too high up.

Easy

> I wrote it down on a list and it went off the list. Then
> I walked by w/o saying hi
> fly on my sleeve. Sixty lines for Ash

Ley.   That rhyme at the start.
We disa
Gree about how to ach
Ieve good   Walking by the pol
Ice car I am bored with my rhymes and
We aren't who
We indicates
We shd
Be together but in this small town our
Trees are far apart and our houses
Be planted next to
Each other well   hello
Wheet-whew cardinal top of tr
Ee   high self-est
Eem as if "survivor"   I don't
Keep enough
Meat on my bones and I'll go
Freely into the soon grinder except I'm
Decently employed at a universit
Y who
Bleeds the ones who can pay
Teases the ones who can't into thinking they've got a good
Deal out the loans   I wander thru
Each charter'd school & mark in ev
Ry eye I
Meet
Weariness and marks of woe   jobbing   Hate this job not
Because I don't enjoy it but
Because I don't
Be
Lieve it's doing an

Y one an
Y good I am not
Meeting my own or an
Yone's
Needs or
Requirements   am
Even sicker of
Meeting them. My failure to come up with a
Creative Solution to
These problems that not everyone
Sees as problems
Is the most uninteresting
Piece of the stor
Y.
He, I worr
Y is down I love him [son and heir]
He has Animal eyes
Be okay night brow   for
We
     have /have n 't
                "we"
Been able Been popular
  Been white Been castled Been way in debt
Been poor Been to college Been
no one died for   link child
       baseball gram   hi cat what you want
Been alive for   figure it out in wire crumple graph

Thanksgiving is over

for Sarah

The South won the civil was. Kept it alive.
We have to read the noose.

I don't wish to won the civil
was, because
the civil wasn't.

Then their was
the reconstruct.
Through which
I came out ahead.

I came out as dead
Was dead at work.

"I'd feel better if you
deserved what you got
when what you got was shit."

Thanksgiving is over.
We don't have to be grateful any more.

Poets try

lewd changes of scale,
synthetic-fleshly phrasebots
economies of binary and scalar
adjustment, clashing gears
to arrest the mind machine
and call that style

and/or make sure
what shouldn't go into a poem   should go in
and what shouldn't be the form
of the poem   should be its form
and what shouldn't be the
venue for the poem
should be its venue   and the poem
should be the host for   disease
the poem should be   debt
a promise   that the current and the
given are unfinished
and when the poet is embarrassed about privilege
the poem can market guilt

Impersonal lubricant

If you're not part of
the solution, dis

solve for x: turn into oyster—
filter phosphates, nitrates, ammonia,

bacteria, plankton into
pellets of harmless nitrogen.

Be brilliant machine.
Keep water clean.

But when the sea turns acid
I can't build my shell!

≡

Signs of aging on my human body
are live gifs of the Age.

My boyfriend's visiting
so I feed the gifs to private

spermcast. Later, wakeful,
I troll for massive breasts

online, find pictures of Denise
Milani and the two huge jellies

sewed onto her chest.
"Denise Milani" once seduced

a brilliant physics professor
into smuggling drugs.

The real Milani did not swindle him.
She knew naught of him.

But her grand breasts
each bigger than her head—

struck from the float
and put to nonconsensual

work in pixel form—
just knocked him out.

≡

Live jellies have no brains,
float blindly

but they can fall asleep, can shed
nerve toxins to defend the colony

and triggered by light
at dawn or dusk

their see-thru pump-domes
simulcast eggs and sperm

into tolerant solution.
Sexual jellies. Some jellyfish

invisible by day
do phosphoresce in darkness.

They could [be] hurt [you]
if you mined them

for the phosphorus
that burns the skin in war.

≡

I am a poet so I
light and gelatin from varied sources

synth, sample rain or
reign, stop wheel

at any point in cycle
to gel my case.

Every oh 21 days now
the eggs come down

in case of use,
last chances to conceive,

cycle speeds up, egg
drop soup my unused protein floats

down sewer to sea, eventually to be
sucked into animal construction.

≡

Researchers built a working jellyfish
of silicon and rat-heart muscle

to test heart meds: a fat lab boob
you can't suck on, professor,

nor milk for gelid silicone
nonreactive.

Rub your cock till it gets hard, professor—
pigs can't do that! only primates

manually self-stim
their privates. I watch an infomercial

in which a male hand strokes a boar's crotch
till eighteen-inch cock unfurls,

fat drinking straw for "milking" sperm.
The boar would prefer a sow in heat

but the sows are in jail
so the male hand

snaps plastic vagina (lined with plastic
bag) onto the cock

and leaves the boar
in private. The boar cums

for some minutes. Fills big bag.
Gate opens. Boar departs.

Male hand removes vagina from its clamp
on metal sawhorse sow.

Pigs left to mate at will might mate
with pigs that don't yield prime bacon,

might mate with sexy pigs, jovial
pigs, smart pigs.

≡

A strange boar's cream
puffs up the chosen sow.

My nerves aglow,
not sexually though

it's gonna take awhile to get me going
couple weeks till ovulation. So

I ogle purple pictures—here's a
wet bead curtain blowing—

a portuguese man-o'-war, blue
siphonophore, see-thru

colonial organism that can clone itself.
In sea-solution

critter drifts
held down

by massive swelling
sea-meniscus

not consensually
not nonconsensually.

Fact Plantation

So folded, tired, I will sing the differences
between plant and plantation
and factory and fact.

Plant and factory are synonyms
(plant has more meanings).
Fact and plantation aren't.
The plantation is a technology
invented by the Portuguese and
exported across the world.
A fact is a unit of meaning
presumed to be known to be true.
Plantations grew and sold
cotton, coffee, tobacco,
sugar, tea, babies
and on those grounds
at the plantation grammar school
(which was a theoretical establishment)
questions would come up, like can nouns speak
if they aren't possessive? and
what's a possessive noun, a white person?

Plant and factory
are synonyms. They name
economies of growth.
Some nouns code activity
in suffixes: plant-*ation*, fact-*ory*.
Other nouns abide
as objects in their manners: desk.
Action-coded nouns
can operate upon their modifiers
(*shoe factory*)
in ways that *desk* cannot.
Witness: in *shoe desk*,
nothing happens

to the shoe, but even we
can be remade
in a *we factory*.
I don't like this plant
factation session. Where to
plant the factory.
Closer to the others.
It makes a stink.

Fact plantation
is synonymous with
intellectual property.
Has date of expiry.
Hap the coming sunstorms
will spark a new ice age
to congeal wet warming globe
so humans live.
What do you
future science know.
Will you be
the end of fact plantation.

At the end of fact plantation
we'll see and you
and when we end
("see you!")
you'll see we end
if you are not the we
that this we was.

July

Just meet you somewhere do it?
  No not in freedom   Why

Keep switching fantasies
Till I get off
  Boss-employee
  Teacher-student

A technique, a rhetoric
Of scale clash (familiar in poems)

Pond trembles like an old projection
Glitter principle:

 Create a bumpy
 Moving surface   cast light on it

Attract attention thus

To make a glittery poem
I need dark
Overlaid with a moving nearly transparent
  Surface that rubbles/rucks
As it grows hillocks
 Snags the light

 — Well that's conventional
Poem — dark "meaning" substrate
While language-tissue wriggles in patterns

If I reached you on the inside of your head
 Red walnut-pod seed crack
 Basal ganglion

Cock rose   my mouth on it
And you were not at all in danger
I was only inside your head with what everyone told me

Later when I thought about you coming
A thin muscle jerked inside my heart

If you need to be punished I will
Punish you   If you want to be
I would rather hold you tenderly

The city has sex with everything

The city has sex

with Kroger.
All over the city, along the white-paint lines that separate parked cars,
 parking lots are unzipping.
 Between the lines, the cars begin to bounce a bit, like babies,
and from the white lines as they widen and crack and split
 a milky fescue grows, reedy wet pathways, little streams
 roseate with lilies, and the streams uprift the concrete
    in grand dispersing E-shapes, and now across the lot
      the broken lines extend until they meet—
    the cars are islanded, really bouncing now
 and Kroger opens all its doors—
  there's a big sale on—
  "big sale" is how the Kroger understands itself to be consenting
to the city tendril-tunneling its homeless homefree energy into the
                                          produce wing—
   the products rapt and blooming breaking open—
plastic-wrap unravels on the floor—a cashier lies down in an
                              expanding crack—
        the milk in there is geothermal warm,
                          it bathes the cashier's nipples,
              he wafts his hands along the reeds like baby Moses
and the Pharaoh's daughter who discovers him is fluorescent light
 reshaping itself (now that the ceiling's gone) into a floating
                              peaceful missile
       congealed of all the city people's formerly constrained mutual care.
          Their energy makes the fluorescence glow like an oil puddle
            ridged in night and sun and opaque peacock fur
until the love missile (which is Pharaoh's daughter flow-light)
  sparks like an old engine
  and ducks and dives
      plays with its comet mates
  caresses them in cloud and basking sun
and then remembers the cashier

lowers its soft missilic body, takes him
into its foggy spider-lightning womb
  he closes his eyes
  and plans to lead the people
 but the cloud-missile says rest
and they listen to percussion—
      rows of imprisoned motley foodlike items
   exploding in a fireworky mess, and the stray dogs
   who lap at Kroger's floor, soft-tonguing, and chew her meat.

The city doesn't just have sex like humans.
It has sex like jellyfish, in a wet cloud
of eggs and sperm released at dusk,
  and like ducks, pushing a hook into a twisted alleyway
  to trap the sperm it doesn't want in a special drawer.
    And it reproduces by cloning, like marbled crayfish,
      which are a female-only species—
      wait, what's a female city that's a clone?
      well it's an imaginary city, it reproduces
      asexually, as mushrooms do, laying out underground throughways
    for clean water and gray water and feces and rain
    and under skyscrapers
  where the soft insides of vehicles wait for humans
 going home alone, rising through
 lit caveways to the highway, the imaginary city
   cares for its parts and members, or the parts and members that are city
   reproduce themselves and one another, look through the shield,
    go ahead you got here first.

The city has sex with Turtle Island
Turtle Island might not want to have sex with it
Will the city have sex with it anyway
The city did

How do you unrape Total Island

Total Island isn't a thing

It is when it's totaled

Totaled = still a thing

Just one you can't pay money for

The city has sex through high-performance industrial screens
Rotex Corp (across Crawford from the cemetery) makes them.
The screens are used for separating minerals, gravel, grains and such.
All the machines feature the exclusive Gyratory Reciprocating Motion.

Gyratory Reciprocating Motion
separates us into categories.
Has a way of doing so.
The city folds along red lines
so it can fuck itself.

This one is hot
because the police have all those extra cocks.
 The cars, the guns. So much
  to come. Such uniform
    containment of our fun
     from they who once like you
      did put their big toe in the bathtub tap
      while dreaming in a bubble bath.
       So many cocks impolitic and impolite
        and weeping from their eyes—
     when the city says Surprise
    and the cop-car drivers' seats
   begin to insinuate themselves
    into the creases of cop asses—
     the seats lean back
     and let the police rest
    while encasing them in
soft and civil flesh, so warm
 their uniforms decay to rags—
see their cocks still weeping
tough, now see their guns endure
  a gentle bris, the guns' foreskins peel back
  exposing the soft fear,
the city kisses it, enfolds it
 in its welcoming warm
  interior skin, the interior of
   everyone in town who
    loved in dark who loved
     in parks who put their world
     in park and made love drive a
     gleaming dirty puddle through
    its vascular connections
     underground together we hold the
      gun's exposed soft penis-fear
     so gently and so lovingly
      that even the rich think they will be OK.

The city has sex on the interstate
Now fill the long tray of I-75 with compost and plant it with grapes
and corn and small dark beans, cucumber frames, playgrounds, a hut
for resting gardeners by the Ezzard Charles exit. Shape the gray air in
the West Side underpass into broad windowed housing—communal
nurseries and kitchens, spiral stairways rising to the highway. Flood the
football stadium with river water. Trout swim past the empty seats.

On the city's intercourse with the city

And if a city is reformulated land,
    what formula
       allows it to consent and seek consent?

    Who owns the city?
   Who'll give the city to the people
        as a present?   Fuck that,

just start unraping it.

The city has sex in private
There is a feeling, when you press my interior grapes, that I am
under a great threat and something very bad is going to happen, as if a
G string on a cheap violin was vibrating so hard it would snap at one
end of its arc of frequency, I will fly off the swing and break my face.
But the G's drone, firm-tethered to my brain and to the plenary panel in
the orchestra pit, rocks on, I can align with it, I will not be thrown, this
took some learning and some practice. Similarly the city if it is to find its
pleasure-zones must risk unbuttoning its proper
boundaries
  grow bright mushrooms
in the dank pits of its ownership
    and let the undocked citizenry talk.

I read and speak
 in signals chemical
  I tremble when the wind collects and moves
  my dew into the storm
I work my sugar-pump
 and calculate from sun and soil-data
  when to split open my
   compressed zipped files
  what do you smell?
  It's what I told you
  not just pleasure
   I told you what I knew.

The city has sex with citizens who fly and crawl
We learn to move, a cloud of microbes
  moves with us, issued from our asses
    in edible (though not to) cucumbers;
      the plants talk to us in smells, though we don't speak their la—
    we divide our speaking into
  units to be caught, repeated,
Animal Microphone in
coyote/bird, at sunrise we receive and bark
  multi-messages in the cacophony and then on
with the day.

Speech by a flaneur—no a flaneuse
On my face, D. folliculorum are relaxing
like Tenniel caterpillars leaning on mushroom stalks
against the bases of my hair follicles
which provide shelter and shade.
These critters are peculiar to
the ecology of the human face
which I take around the city
open, close   it is my means
of feeding   I rely on
changing its shape
in response to others' faces and postures
to reduce my risk and increase my safety
and my likelihood of being
included in the group's collective
life. I smile a lot and hope it
don't look fake.

when the air shaped like the inverse of Megan
accepts Megan as she moves.

   If Megan is a system of exchange
that floats her labor and her point

 of view in vapor/liquid soup
passàging through her valves

and if her later corpse, collapsing,
 updates its inversion of the air

 even more than did the air displace
when she grew from brown-eyed baby

into strong laboring woman in blue jeans
 and heathered wool,

and if the air and earth draw from Megan's corpse
  all the energy and minerals

 she pulled from her surrounds
to build her nails and bones and teeth—

 if the exchange doesn't stop
but only ceases to support her consciousness,

 and if her consciousness was corpse anyway until
it found relation,

 then what demises
is the potential for the human social

and another sociality
 will…unbutton my whole shoe

and tongue hang limp,
   what sex is for but stops me

at the barrier, a pixellated
glamor reef though very

   close and simple, smell a
   flurry, parapluie paraphrase,

energy funneled through a shape.
You filtered chemical

information in such a pointy
fulgent scrambled way, in the city

   and outside the city in the vernal zones
   and aqua zones the city shaped, flow-charted, realist

trucked. The city caved under
   when the zones rose and lapped around the pilings,

manged foundations green,
   rotted the teeth out of the mouth of the city,

harbor high-rises
dark and blown. The city is extremely fragile tender

human mesh and will be mush
   and mushrooms grow in, there is room in, ruins

roam the rearticulated harm.

Poverty, when defined by income,

Creates only one solution:
working for someone else. So

change the form of the for
for animals and problem-solving

plants. I have borrowed
for the inside of my life

the inside-out of
enslaved people and workers

who made the seen.
What are you going to do without your

underclass, where you going
to go, what are you

going to
do without your

woman.
If a nail is unison

entering into unison is violent.
Thus will I cheat

the rich out of my life.

Improper

Something surreptitious about the
way that furry grass-stand is

 rubbing against itself, blowing
 against itself
 nodding and robbing space.

Acknowledgements

Gratitude to the editors of the following journals where poems in this collection first appeared: *Bennington Review, Brooklyn Rail, Chicago Review, Datableed, 580 Split, Journal of Poetics Research, Lana Turner, Old Pal, Poetry, P-Queue, Recliner, Splinter* and *Split Level.* I wrote the last section of this book during a remarkable year with the Alman "Urban Futures" cohort; thanks to the Humanities Center at Miami University for awarding Iñaki Pradanos and me the Altman Fellowship and to all the brilliant student and faculty members of the cohort. Residencies at Eliot House in Gloucester, Massachusetts and Mount Tremper Arts in Woodstock, New York gave me quiet space for finishing this book (thanks, Mary, Dana Hawkes, and Carter Edwards). Thanks to the members of the Environmental Humanities Research Collaborative (Iñaki Pradanos, Suzanne McCullagh, Ilaria Tabusso Marcyan, and Ryan Gunderson) for galvanizing conversations at Circle Bar. Thanks to Mary Jean Corbett for finding a way to give me time. Thanks to my AAUP co-conspirators—Don and Fran Ucci, Gaile Pohlhaus, David Walsh, Theresa Kulbaga, and especially Deborah Lyons. Thanks to the Cincinnati poet walkers: Pat Clifford, cris cheek, and Tyrone Williams. Many friends read these poems and helped me with them: Judith Goldman, Karen Weiser, Dana Ward, Lewis Freedman, Megan Martin, Charles Gabel, Ashley Colley, Martin Corless-Smith, Rebecca Wolff, and especially Brett Price. Andrew Lorent, thank you for honesty. Strawberrius (and to Schnee in the after-bios) for affectionate interruptions, and to Ambrose for patience and love.